Bratislava Travel Guide

Sightseeing, Hotel, Restaurant & Shopping Highlights

Rebecca Kaye

Copyright © 2014, Astute Press
All Rights Reserved.

No part of this publication may be reproduced, stored in a retrieval system, or transmitted, in any form or by any means without the prior written permission of the publisher, nor be otherwise circulated in any form of binding or cover other than that in which it is published and without similar condition being imposed on the subsequent purchaser.

If there are any errors or omissions in copyright acknowledgements the publisher will be pleased to insert the appropriate acknowledgement in any subsequent printing of this publication.

Although we have taken all reasonable care in researching this book we make no warranty about the accuracy or completeness of its content and disclaim all liability arising from its use

Table of Contents

Bratislava 5
   Culture 7
   Location & Orientation 9
   Climate & When to Visit 11

Sightseeing Highlights 13
   Bratislava Castle 13
   Grassalkovich Palace 16
   Michael's Gate 17
   Main Square & Old Town Hall 19
   Old Town Street 20
   Slavin War Memorial 22
   Novy Most (New Bridge) 23
   St Martin's Cathedral 24
   Primate's Palace 25
      Slovak National Museum 26

Recommendations for a Budget Traveller 28
   Places to Stay 28
      Falkensteiner Hotel Bratislava 28
      Hotel SET 29
      Hotel Matsyak 29
      Hotel Abba 30
      Austria Trend Hotel 30
   Places to Eat 31
      UFO 31
      Slovak Pub 31
      Altitude Restaurant 32
      Antica Toscana 32
      Hradna Hviezda 33
   Places to Shop 33
      Old Town Christmas Market 33
      Aupark Shopping Center 34
      Polus City Center 34
      Old Town 34
      Obchodna Street 35

Bratislava

Bratislava on the Danube River is an often under-rated city that offers historic palaces, a medieval Old Town, and an interesting set of churches, museums and art galleries. It is the capital and largest city of Slovakia. Located in the southwest of the country, Bratislava is under one hour's drive from Vienna and is the only national capital in the world that borders two other countries (Hungary and Austria).

It occupies both the banks of the popular Danube River and fans out on the left bank of the Morava River.

The city was founded before the 10th century and has been an important seat of power for many kingdoms and states that it has been a part of. Bratislava was a part of the Hungarian kingdom from the 10th century until the World War I. Between the 16th and the mid 19th centuries, Bratislava was the capital and the coronation city of the Kingdom of Hungary. During World War II, it was part of the German-controlled state. Later with the formation of Czechoslovakia it became the capital of the Federal State of Slovakia, until the formation of Slovakia as an independent country in 1993, when it was declared the capital of the independent nation.

The Hungarian influence on the city is evident from the fact that its original name is Hungarian – Pozsony. By the 19th and early 20th century the city was known by its German (or, as some say, Austrian) name Pressburg. The city got its present name Bratislava, as late as 1919.

Due to its importance in the medieval ages, Bratislava has mentions in many other European languages, each in their own form and dialect. However, one that stands out is the Greek name Istrapolis which translates to Danube City, a reference to the famous River Danube which passes through the city and has numerous citations in poems, literary works, and music pieces over the centuries.

Bratislava is a very small city and is often a day-trip for many visitors from the neighboring countries. The historic Old Town is not only the center of the city; it is also the major attraction with all major tourist spots in or around the area.

It can be covered easily in a day. In spite of this small size, Bratislava has been able to attract visitors from central Europe and beyond for its picturesque medieval streets, scenic natural beauty, and over a dozen historic palaces and churches spread all over the city.

Culture

For a city the size of Bratislava, there are ample opportunities for entertainment all the year round. From classical concerts to wild bachelor parties, the city has it all. With its close proximity to Vienna, Bratislava has a strong influence of classical music. It is home to Slovak Philharmonic Orchestra and the Capella Istropolitana – a popular ensemble of chamber music. Birthplace to Johann Hummel and Franz Schmidt, and host to masters like Beethoven, Liszt, and Haydn.

Bratislava has an enviable history of western classical music. Each year, the city hosts the popular Bratislava Music Festival and the Bratislava Jazz Days. The annual Wilsonic Festival attracts crowds and artists from different European countries. Summer times see a lot of the music acts being held at the Bratislava Castle and the parks around Old Town.

Theater lovers can visit the 1000-seat Old Slovak National Theater. Housed in a late 19th century building on the riverfront at the edge of the Old Town, just the visit to the building is an experience in itself. It used to be illuminated with 800 gas lamps.

The interiors are beautifully decorated with frescoes and paintings. A new Slovak National Theater with 1700 seats was opened in 2007 and is also near the Danube waterfront. Both these theaters host opera, ballet and drama. The city has a number of smaller theaters like the Arena Theatre, L+S Theatre, Naïve Theatre, and the Astorka Korzo Theatre.

Bratislava has a number of annual festivals, from cultural to culinary. Popular amongst those are the Bratislava Ball (January), City Marathon (March or April), Easter Market (April), Wine Festival (May), Junifest Beer Festival (June), and the Christmas Market (December). Reenactments of historic Slovak events can be seen at many annual events like the Seize of Bratislava (June), Coronation Celebration (1st weekend every September), and the Festival of Historic Fencing (July & August).

The city is also famous and, at times, infamous for its nightlife. Known to be inexpensive and liberal – highlighted in the popular teen movie Eurotrip in 2004 – the city has attracted many parties from revelers from the city as well as neighboring countries. Popular night clubs in the city include the Loft!, Barrock, Subclub, and the Trafo Music Bar. However, the city is not only about loud wild partying; one can enjoy a drink and local band in many of the pubs and bars in town. Many of these are close to the Old Town. Some of the popular spots include Slovak Pub, Jazz Café, Dubliner Pub, El Diablo Pub, and the Cocoloco Cocktail Bar.

Location & Orientation

The beautiful medieval town of Bratislava is blessed with the proximity to many major Central European cities, making it ideal for 1-2 day trip. It is closest to the Austrian capital, Vienna (about 60 km), making the 2 cities the 2 closest capital cities in Europe. It is about 150 km from Budapest and Graz, and less than 300 km from Zagreb, Prague, Kosice, Warsaw, and Ljubljana. Although the city has a full-fledged working international airport, the close proximity with these neighboring cities and the good condition of the European highways make it ideal to be accessed by road.

The city is served by the Bratislava Milan Rastislav Štefánik Airport (IATA: BTS). The airport is located on the eastern part of the city and is linked through the D1 motorway. With the introduction of low cost carriers, it has been able to draw a considerable number of tourists, especially the younger crowd from the neighboring countries and the UK. The airport is connected to the city through bus and taxi service. Bus no. 61 (to the main railway station in the city), No. 91 (to Petrzalka), and night-bus N61 are available near the Departure terminal. Tickets have to be bought before boarding from the kiosks or manned-counters at the airport. Whereas the bus ticket costs about €1, taxis are much more expensive and could cost up to €30 for a trip to the city center.

For those who are flying in to central Europe can also use the Vienna International Airport (IATA: VIE) – http://www.viennaairport.com/jart/prj3/va/main.jart which is located about 40 km from Bratislava. Regular bus connections (by Postbus and Blaguss) connect the airport with Bratislava. With less than €10 for a ticket, it is a good option for travelers flying in from other continents as there are better and cheaper connections to Vienna.

Bratislava has 2 main train stations – Bratislava hlavn astanica and Bratislava-Petrzalka. Both the stations are well connected by the public bus service. Vienna is just an hour away and is connected by the regional express service twice daily. Prague (4 hrs), Berlin (9 hrs), Budapest (3 hrs), Warsaw (8 hrs), and Belgrade (11 hrs) are connected by the EC train service with multiple daily connections.

With excellent motorways, Bratislava is often accessed by road. In fact, due to the closeness of some of the neighboring major cities, it is actually quicker to take the bus than taking the flight. Major inter-country bus services like Slovak Lines, Eurolines, Orange ways, and Blaguss have multiple connections with Bratislava from not only the neighboring cities, but also from cities as far away as London and Paris. Tickets can be bought at the bus stations or online. It is recommended to buy the tickets in advance, especially for weekend travel and during peak tourist season, as many of these buses get fully booked. Some of the bus services come with in-built toilet, free Wi-Fi, and a beverage counter (against payment) making the travel very comfortable. All long distance buses stop at the Central Terminal (Auto busovastanica) which has trolley-bus and bus connections to different parts of Bratislava.

For those planning to drive, it is necessary to get a vignette (sticker) - to be put on the windshield - once the car enters the Slovakia limits. The vignette can be bought at any gas station. In the city there are 'Park and Walk' facilities. Parking is also available near the city center (the Old Town is auto free zone) but it may be difficult to find a parking space in the narrow one way streets of Bratislava. Kiosks and parking attendants (wearing yellow vests) are available to buy the parking tickets from.

Located on the banks of the Danube, Bratislava is connected by boat services with Vienna. High speed ferry services run daily and cost about €30 for a return ticket.

Once in the city, most of it can easily be covered by foot. Public transport is available through the bus, trolley bus and tram service. Tickets must be bought before boarding and must be validated at the start of the journey. Public transport is also available during the night. A good option for tourists is to buy the Bratislava City Card - http://visit.bratislava.sk/en/vismo/zobraz_dok.asp?id_org=700014&id_ktg=1102&p1=6492.

Climate & When to Visit

Bratislava has a moderately continental climate. It is the sunniest and warmest part of the country with low to moderate rainfall spread all year round. Summer months between April and September have an average high of about 24 degrees Celsius and an average low of about 12 degrees.

Winter months between October and March see an average high of about 7 degrees Celsius and an average low just below freezing. Although the city, especially the Old Town, is beautifully lit up during the Christmas months, it is the summer months that attract most of the tourists to Bratislava for the dry and comfortable weather conditions.

Sightseeing Highlights

Bratislava Castle

Tel: +421 2 544 114 44

Originally built in the 9th century, the Bratislava Castle, perched on a hill on the bank of the River Danube is the most dominating structure on the city skyline. Due to its location on the Little Carpathians rocky hilltop, one can get excellent panoramic views of the city as well as parts of Austria and Hungary from the castle premises. It was declared a National Cultural Monument in 1961 (before the birth of the present day independent country of Slovakia).

Although there are no clear records of the first construction of the castle, it is believed that the castle hill was inhabited from the ancient times. People from the Boleraz culture inhabited there and used a fortified settlement for their protection. Its strategic location made the castle hill an important settlement for the Celts and the Romans until the 5th century AD. About 400 years later – around the 9th century AD during the occupation by the Slavs, a large stone castle was built on the castle hill. Under the Kingdom of Hungary, the city started gaining political and commercial importance and the castle was recognized as one of the major seats of power in the kingdom.

Renovations and expansions went on for the next few centuries with the castle getting a Romanesque as well as Gothic architectural look. During the middle ages it was known as the Pressburg Castle. In the 15th century, there were major rearrangements of the castle and the only surviving part today from the original plan is the Sigismund Gate – popularly known as the Corvinus Gate. Renaissance changes in the early 17th century brought a Baroque look to some parts of the castle. In the 2nd half of the 18th century, the castle was the home to Queen Maria Theresa of the Kingdom of Hungary. Interiors were changed and given a rococo-style finish. Gradients of the stairs were also changed so that the queen could ride her horse through the stairways!

By the early 19th century the castle fell into major disrepair. The 2 world wars saw the castle being used as army barracks. An amphitheater was built in the castle premises. In the mid 1950s a 10-year restoration was done to bring back the glory of the castle.

In the years that followed, the Bratislava Castle was used for many state receptions. A further €50 million was approved in 2008 for restoration of the castle. Although restoration work is ongoing, the castle is open to the public for free and visitors have access to many parts of the castle and the courtyard.

The present castle is a huge rectangular building in white with 4 towers at the 4 corners. The roofs and tower tops are in orange giving the castle a distinct bright look on the green hilltop. There are 4 gates to enter the castle although Leopold Gate is no more accessible. The Sigismund Gate – built in the 15th century – is the oldest gate and is on the southeast of the castle. It is the most used gate for those walking for the Old Town. The Vienna Gate is on the southwest and is accessible through the Palisady Street. This gate is used for those who come by bus or car. The Nicholas Gate on the northwest has the steepest climb through a number of stairs on the hillside. This gate is used by those who come from the Danube riverside.

To the west of the main castle building is the reconstructed 18th century Hillebrandt building. The open space just in front of the castle gates is the Court of Honor. The east of the castle has the 9th century Great Moravian Basilica and the 11th century Church of St Savior. If entering through the Nicholas Gate, one goes through a Gothic gateway that dates back to the 15th century. The Baroque stable at the side of the courtyard has been transformed into a restaurant. The northern border of the castle has an 18th century building that houses the Historical Museum section of the Slovak National Museum.

Grassalkovich Palace

Located in the Hodzovo Square, to the north of the Old Town, is the Presidential Palace or the Grassalkovich Palace. Built in 1760, the palace has a rococo and baroque architectural style and is named after Count Antal Grassalkovich, the head of the Hungarian Chamber for the Kingdom of Hungary. With a French garden on the outside and beautiful rooms, decorated chapel, and a grand staircase on the inside, the palace is one of the most beautiful buildings in the Slovak capital. It is the official residence of the President of Slovakia.

This impressive palace was designed by architect Anton Mayerhofer. The garden at the back of the palace has a statue of Queen Maria Theresa riding a horse. There is also a beautiful Fountain of Youth by noted Slovak sculptor – Tibor Bartfay. Avant-garde statues by various other contemporary sculptors can also be seen in the garden. There is a statue of noted composer Jan Nepomuck Hummel. The garden is open to the public from dawn till sundown. With dogs and bicycles not allowed in the garden, it has become a popular kid's playground. The garden can be accessed through the Banskobrystrická Street and the Stefanikova Street.

The palace was a center for many public gatherings and musical performances in the late 18th century. As Anton was an advisor to Queen Theresa, the palace was used for many royal parties and balls. Joseph Haydn, the legendary composer, was a favorite of Prince Esterhazy, and premiered many of his musicals in this palace.

After the end of World War I, the palace came under the control of the Territorial Military Command. During World War II, it was the seat of the President of the Slovak Republic. After the War, for a few years (1945 to 1950) it was the seat for the ruling Communists. In 1950 the palace was made an activity center for the schoolchildren of Bratislava. The building was extensively damaged by the schoolchildren but renovation was only possible after the end of the Communist rule in 1989. After major reconstructions in the first half of the 1990s, the palace was declared as the official residence of the Slovak President on September 1996.

Michael's Gate

Built sometime around 1300, Michael's Gate is the oldest city gate from the medieval fortifications of Bratislava. It is one of the oldest preserved buildings and stands as one of the gates to the Old Town. It went through major reconstruction in 1758 when it was a given a Baroque look along with a bulbous tower top and a statue of St Michael with the Dragon. Today, standing at 51m, the tower is home to the Weapons Museum section of the Bratislava City Museum.

The entrance to the town (now the Old Town) was heavily fortified in the middle ages. There were 4 heavily fortified gates that controlled the entry and exit. The east of the town had the Laurinc Gate.

To the west was the Fishermen's Gate (as it was mostly used by fishermen who used to bring their catch from the River Danube). To the west was Vydrica Gate or the Black Gate, so named as it was almost in the form of a tunnel. To the north was the Michael's Gate, the only one to have survived the passage of time. It was named after the St Michael's Church that was in front of it. The church was pulled down to finance the extension of the town walls.

In its early years, the gate at St Michael's used to have a drawbridge over a moat for security. A stone bridge later replaced the moat, a structure that stands to date and must be crossed to enter the Old Town through the St Michael's Gate. The gate itself had large wooden doors. For nearly 200 years, newly coronated Hungarian Kings would enter the town through the Vydrica Gate for their coronation and then come to St Michael's Gate to take a pledge of monarchy in the hands of the state's archbishop.

Today, the 7-storey tower houses the Weapons Museum that displays the fortification history of the city. The building, reconstruction, and finally the destruction of the town walls are explained through various exhibits. The 6th floor has a viewing platform from where one can have excellent panoramic views of the Old Town. The street that passes through the St Michel's Gate has a 'zero kilometer plate' and lists the distances of 29 world capitals from that point.

Main Square & Old Town Hall

Certainly one of the most popular tourist spots in the Old Town and home to the Bratislava Christmas Market, the Main Square is located right in the middle of the Old Town. It is dominated by the Old Town Hall and the Roland Fountain that is located on the southwestern corner of the square. Beautiful uniformly colored medieval buildings surround the square. Home to many foreign embassies, these beautiful buildings create a very cheerful ambience to the Old Town center. Cultural programs and concerts are held in the Main Square during the summer months.

The Old Town Hall which stands at the eastern flank of the Main Square is actually a complex of buildings. The buildings and the tower date back to the 14th century, making it one of the oldest stone buildings and the oldest city hall in Slovakia. Three townhouses and a palace were merged to create the present day Town Hall. The buildings that were merged were the Jacobus House (with the tower), the Pawer House, the Unger House, and the Aponyi Palace. The tower, during the early years, used to have a mechanical clock, a sphere showing the phases of the moon, and bells. Today the tower has 4 clock faces and a viewing platform with a 360 degree view of the Old Town. The buildings have gone through several reconstructions and renovations over the years and have a variety of architectural styles – gothic, baroque, neo-renaissance, and neo-gothic. The Town hall is home to the city's oldest museum, the Bratislava City Museum (1868).

The merged buildings were used as the Town Hall until the late 19th century. The buildings also served many other purposes. It was used as a prison, a mint, a municipal archive, and an arsenal depository.

The Weapons Museum in the Town Hall has many interesting exhibits. One of the most popular is a cannonball shot by Napoleon's army in 1809 during their attack on Petrzalka; the cannonball, to this day, is stuck in the tower wall! Other exhibits include medieval torture instruments, armors, weapons, old town dungeons, and some paintings and miniatures. The building, which was originally the Aponyi Palace, is used as a study of Glass and Ceramics.

Old Town Street

A walk though the Old Town of Bratislava is not just a visual treat with the beautiful colored medieval buildings and cobbled streets; it is made interesting and exciting through many quirky statues that have become a major attraction with the visitors.

Rubberneck, or Cumil, is the bronze statue of a man peeking out of a sewerage hole. It is one of the most photographed attractions in the Slovak capital. There is a sign warning oncoming drivers about the statue as it had lost its head twice to reckless drivers. Rubberneck can be seen at the corner of Rybarskabrana, at the junction of Sedlarska and Panska streets.

The Schoner Naci bronze statue is on the Sedlarska Street. This life size statue by Juraj Melus is dedicated to Ignac Lamar, the grandson of a clown who used to walk in the streets of Old Town in the mid 20th century, greeting people and trying to make them smile. Mentally ill but much loved he used to survive on free food given by many of the cafes and restaurants in Old Town. He passed away in 1967; his remains were brought to Bratislava where he was reburied in 2007.

The Paparazzi bronze statue is on Laurinska Street. Dressed in an overcoat and top hat, he is seen aiming his full lens camera from the corner of a building at passers-by.

Located on the Main Square is the bronze statue of Napoleon's Soldier. The statue of this fully uniformed French soldier leans on a bench in the square and provides ample opportunities to be photographed with.

A unique and mischievous stone sculpture can be seen on 29 Panska Street. Located on top of an optician store, it shows a naked man peaking out of a window. There have been many versions to explain the statue; some say he is rushing out so as not to miss the coronation whereas others say that he is mocking a neighbor who used to spy on passersby.

Slavin War Memorial

Commemorating Bratislava's liberation by the Russian Red Army in April 1945, the Slavin War Memorial is a gigantic war memorial that is visible from many parts of the city. Located on a hilltop north of the Bratislava Castle, and standing nearly 50m high, the war memorial is also the cemetery to 6845 Russian soldiers who died in the final weeks of World War II while fighting to free Bratislava and its neighboring regions.

The memorial was designed by Jan Svetlik and opened to the public in 1960 on the 15th anniversary of the liberation of the city. It was declared a National Cultural Monument a year later. The impressive memorial has a central obelisk which rises 39m; this is topped by the statue of a victorious soldier carrying the Soviet flag, which rises another 11m in height. There is a bronze door that opens into the memorial auditorium. The central solemn hall has a number of statues and inscriptions; there is also a white marble sarcophagus. The base of the memorial has the inscriptions of the names of the Slovak cities that were liberated by the Russian Red Army during their westward advance in the last 2 years of the World War II.

The memorial symbolizes the gratitude the Slovaks had towards the Russians for liberating them from the German Wehrmacht units. However, the relations soured considerably when the Soviet backed Communist Party ousted Alexander Dubcek, the popular Slovak leader, and gained control of Czechoslovakia in the late 1940s.

Today, the war memorial, located in one of the wealthier districts of Bratislava with foreign embassies and rich residences, is a great place for a relaxed stroll. The panoramic views of the city from the memorial are spectacular making the memorial a must-visit place, especially on a clear sunny day.

Novy Most (New Bridge)

The Most Slovenskéhonárodnéhopovstania (which translates to Bridge of the Slovak National Uprising or Most SNP), commonly known as the Novy Most or New Bridge is on the River Danube connecting the southern part of the Old Town to Petrzalka on the south bank of Bratislava. The bridge was originally named Most SNP in 1972; the name was changed to New Bridge in 1993, and then changed back to Most SNP on August 2012.

Completed in 1972, after a 5-year construction, the bridge ranks 32nd in the World Federation of Great Towers; making it the shortest tower as well as the only bridge in the rankings. The Most SNP is the longest cable stayed bridge in the world which has a single pylon and one cable-stayed plane. The Most SNP stretches 430.8 m (the main span on the water is 303 m) in length and has a steel construction that is suspended from steel cables.

The Most SNP is easily identifiable by the 84.6 m pylon near the Petrzalka end of the bridge; on top of the pylon is a flying saucer-shaped restaurant.

Originally called the Bystrica, it was renamed UFO in 2005 prompting many people to call the Most SNP, the UFO Bridge. The east pillar of the pylon has an elevator reaching up to the restaurant that has excellent views of the River Danube and both banks of the Slovak capital. The west pillar has a 430-step staircase for emergency evacuation. The bridge itself has 2 levels, the upper level is open to motor traffic and has 4 lanes, and the lower level is for bicycles and pedestrians.

St Martin's Cathedral

One of the most common photographs of Bratislava is from the Bratislava Castle hilltop overlooking the Old Town skyline. The most dominating tower (spire) of the skyline is that of the St Martin's Cathedral, a 15th century Catholic cathedral. Affiliated to the Roman Catholic Archdiocese of Bratislava, it is the largest and one of the oldest churches in the city. It is of great historical importance. Located on the southwestern boundary of the Old Town, the church was a part of the medieval fortifications. It was also the coronation church to the Kingdom of Hungary. Between 1563 and 1860, the coronation parade would enter through the Black Gate on the west wall, go to the St Martin's Cathedral for the coronation, and then head to the St Michael's Gate for the oath to the state's archbishop.

The cathedral with its 85 m tall spire is built in a classic crucifix shape. The top of the spire has a 300-kg gilded replica of the Hungarian Royal crown.

The nave of the cathedral has 3 aisles. It is built amidst a spacious courtyard with cobblestoned side-streets. Beautiful stained-glass windows adorn the interior.

The original church was in the neighboring Bratislava Castle but had to be shifted out in the 13th century for security reasons to the spot where the present cathedral is. Originally a Romanesque church was built but was replaced by a bigger and new Gothic cathedral that was commissioned in the early 14th century. Construction was completed in the mid 15th century – in 1452. The church and the spire had gone through numerous renovations and reconstructions over the centuries due to many disasters – fire, lightning, earthquake, as well as war. Parts of the St Martin's Cathedral were restructured to build the Most SNP which has its northern end in front of the cathedral.

Primate's Palace

Located in the Old Town is the impressive late 18th century neo-classical building, the Primate's Palace. Originally built for the Archbishop, it is today the seat of the Bratislava Mayor. The palace has a north facing façade built in a classical style of architecture. The roof has a number of allegorical statues depicting the different human qualities and achievements. On the top of the tympanum is the coat of arms of the first occupant of the palace – Cardinal Jozef Batthyanyi. A 150-kg iron model of the cardinal's hat crowns the top of the palace.

One of the most popular halls in the palace is the Hall of Mirrors. The early 19th century Treaty of Bratislava between Austria and France was signed in the Hall of Mirrors. Nowadays, the hall is used to host concerts. The city purchased the Primate's Palace in 1903 and during a reconstruction the same year, rare 17th century English tapestry produced in the English town of Mortlake was discovered inside the palace. The Hall of Mirrors and the tapestry are open for public viewing making the palace worth a visit when in Bratislava.

Slovak National Museum

Tel: +421 2 204 69 114
http://www.snm.sk/?home

Established in 1961, the Slovak National Museum is a combination of 18 national museums, 8 of which are located in the capital city, Bratislava. Headquartered in Bratislava, the museum has a total collection of 3894000 objects, which amounts to nearly 40% of the total museum collections in Slovakia. It is the primary institution in Slovakia that is focused on the cultural education and research in museological activity in the country. From ancient every day tools to fancy facilities used by the nobles in the Middle Ages, the different museums have a variety of collections that could interest people from different backgrounds.

The museums located in the city include the Natural Science Museum, Archeological Museum, Museum of History, Music Museum, Museum of Jewish Culture, Museum of Hungarian Culture in Slovakia, Museum of Carpathian German Culture, and the Museum of Croatian Culture in Slovakia.

Recommendations for a Budget Traveller

Places to Stay

Falkensteiner Hotel Bratislava

Pilarikova 5
Bratislava
Tel: +421 2 592 36 100
http://www.falkensteiner.com/en/hotel/bratislava

The Falkensteiner Hotel Bratislava is a 4 star property that is located to the west of the Old Town, near the St Michael's Gate. This stylish modern hotel has a 24 hr reception, VIP room service, and a concierge service. Airport transfers and parking can be arranged by the hotel. There is an onsite restaurant, bar, executive lounge, and snack vending machines. Pets are allowed. There is free Wi-Fi. Rooms are very spacious and equipped with all modern facilities with rates starting from €139.

Hotel SET

Kaliniciakova 29
Nove Mesto, Bratislava
Tel: +421 2 491 09 600
http://en.hotelset.sk/

Located in the Nove Mesto district, Hotel SET is a 4 star property with the National Tennis Center and the hockey stadium in close proximity. This non-smoking property has free Wi-Fi and parking. There is a 24 hr reception. Pets are allowed. There is an onsite restaurant, bar, and ATM machine. Rooms are ensuite and with all modern facilities. Rates start from €48 including breakfast.

Hotel Matsyak

Prazska 15
Bratislava
Tel: +421 2 206 3 4001
http://www.hotelmatysak.sk/home/

This 3 star hotel is located right across the road from the main train station. The closest major attraction is the Slavin War Memorial. There is free parking and a 24 hr front desk. Facilities include onsite restaurant, bar, and currency exchange. There is free LAN internet in the rooms. The specialty of the hotel is the elaborate wine cellar with more than 40000 bottles! Rooms are elegantly decorated with rates starting from €70.

Hotel Abba

Stefanikova 4
Bratislava
Tel: +421 2 5751 1000
http://www.abbabratislavahotel.com/en

Located close to the Slavin War Memorial and the Grassalkovich Palace, the Hotel Abba is a new hotel with modern rooms and excellent facilities which include a 24 hr reception, free Wi-Fi, onsite restaurant, snack bar, bicycle rental, and a travel desk. All the 125 rooms are equipped with the latest convenience with prices starting at €60.

Austria Trend Hotel

Vysoka 2A
Bratislava
Tel: +421 2 52 775 800
http://www.austria-trend.at/hotel-bratislava/en/

This 4 star hotel is located very close to the Grassalkovich Palace. It has 24 hr front desk, VIP room service, and a concierge service. Pets are allowed. There is free Wi-Fi. There is an onsite restaurant and a bar. It also has a sauna and a fitness center. All the 199 rooms are ensuite and have 'every conceivable comfort'. Room rates start from €80.

Places to Eat

UFO

Novy Most (Most SNP)
Bratislava
Tel: +421 2 62 52 0300
http://www.redmonkeygroup.com/

Located on the Most SNP (bridge) on the River Danube, this is one of the most impressive restaurant addresses in Bratislava. The 2-page menu includes a 7-course dinner (€75) and a 3-course lunch (€30). The restaurant also serves a wide variety of wine and spirits. There is a bar located 85m above ground level having excellent panoramic views of the city. The entry fee (€6.50) for the 95m high viewing level is waived for the restaurant guests.

Slovak Pub

Obchodna 62
Bratislava
Tel: +421 2 5263 3285
http://www.slovakpub.sk/

The Slovak Pub is not just a pub but also a full-fledged restaurant, and certainly one of the best places to try authentic Slovak cuisine.

The place has a medieval pub décor with some of the interior pieces dating back nearly 200 years! Main dishes are priced around €5 making it very pocket friendly too, one of the reasons why it may be very crowded in the evenings. The Slovak Pub is located just outside the Old Town.

Altitude Restaurant

Cestana Kamzik 14
Bratislava
Tel: +421 2 4425 69 46
http://www.altitude.sk/?blogs=altitude_uvod&lang=en

Aptly named, this is the highest restaurant in Bratislava and has a 360 degree view of the city. It is located in the 195m high Kamzik TV Tower. Altitude has a brasserie, a restaurant, a passage bar, and a dance hall. European and Slovak cuisine is served with the main dishes priced between €12 & €26. Desserts are priced about €6. Excellent cuisine, great views, and an elegant atmosphere make the visit to the Altitude a great experience.

Antica Toscana

Madarska 27
Bratislava
Tel: +421 2 6285 9307
http://www.anticatoscana.sk/

Open every day except Monday, this is one of the finest Italian restaurants in Bratislava.

It has both indoor and outdoor seating. Waiters are prompt and helpful. It has a big variety of authentic Italian pastas (and risottos) which is specially recommended. This small cozy restaurant uses original Italian spices for the preparation. A full meal costs between €5 and €10.

Hradna Hviezda

Bratislava Castle
Tel: 0944 14 27 18
http://www.hradnahviezda.sk/

This elegantly decorated restaurant is part of the Bratislava Castle. Although the prices are on the higher side, the delicious food and excellent service makes it worth it. It serves various European cuisines like Slovak, English, French, Italian, and German. The prices for the main dishes range between €15 and €20. It also serves wine from the neighboring Carpathian vineyards.

Places to Shop

Old Town Christmas Market

A must-visit market if one is visiting Bratislava in December, the Christmas Market is concentrated at the courtyard in front of the Old Town Hall.

Concerts and light shows keep the place lively every evening. It is the ideal place to not only buy some traditional Slovak gifts but also to try the local mulled wine and potato pancakes.

Aupark Shopping Center

Located in Einsteinova, this modern shopping center has all the convenience and offerings of a modern mall. There is a grocery super market, cinema complex, fitness center, and over 25 different eateries and pubs. There is also a car wash and a children's play area.

Polus City Center

This huge shopping center is located in the Nove Mesto district of the city. It has a shopping center, hypermarket, fitness center, cinema complex, and a post office in its premises. There is also a casino arcade that is open 24 hrs. There are over two dozen places to eat or drink, from fine dining to fast food.

Old Town

The auto free zone inside the Old Town is the ideal place to not only have a stroll on the medieval streets but also to buy varieties of products – from branded items like Gucci and D&G to hand-made crafts of Slovakia. The streets also have many souvenir stores selling a wide variety of products aimed at tourists.

Obchodna Street

Obchodna is one of the most happening streets with plenty of bars and boutique stores. The street leads right up to the St Michael's Gate of the Old Town. On one side of the street there are a number of hostels and budget accommodations. On the other side of the street, along with plenty of restaurants, bars, and ice cream parlors, one can find stores on fashion and accessories. A small lane off the Obchodna leads into a street market where one can buy winter clothes at a bargain.

Printed in Great Britain
by Amazon.co.uk, Ltd.,
Marston Gate.